ALFRED'S DRUM METHOD
BOOK 1

Sandy Feldstein
Dave Black

──────── **ALFRED'S DRUM METHOD DVD** ────────

Add excitement and understanding to your percussion studies with Alfred's Drum Method DVD (#20877). It is an 80-minute instructional DVD featuring lessons with the authors. The DVD correlates directly with Alfred's Drum Method, Book 1 and will guide and motivate your practice time. Each solo is performed by renowned percussionist Jay Wanamaker. The DVD is attractively packaged, well-produced and is an excellent reference tool for teachers, students and university drum method instructors.

──────── **ALFRED'S DRUM METHOD, BOOK 2** ────────

After you have successfully completed book 1, you are ready for book 2 of Alfred's Drum Method (#238). It has been designed to provide a comprehensive approach to assist you in your pursuit of becoming a well-rounded percussionist. Alfred's Drum Method, Book 2 includes materials which explore traditional rudimental style, corps style and orchestral style, plus sections which deal with accessory instruments and multiple percussion techniques. As in book 1, all new ideas are combined in exciting contest-style solos.

FOREWORD

This book is designed to help the student become a fine player while also providing how-to knowledge regarding drum care, drum tuning, plus stick and drum head selection. It will give him/her a sound musical background while providing for the highest degree of interest and motivation. Each page is designed as a complete lesson; materials are combined at the end of each lesson in a logical and musical solo passage. There is also an entire drum solo at the end of each complete section which may be used for contest purposes.

The method also includes actual drum parts from well known marches. Although some have been edited so they can be played by the beginning student, they remain musically faithful to the original band pieces. Students may wish to play along with the numerous available recordings of these classic marches.

The student must set aside a reasonable amount of practice time on a regular basis in order to achieve best results. He/she should play each exercise as written, being certain that proper hand, finger, arm, and body positions are maintained at all times.

The authors have made certain to present the material in an enjoyable and interesting manner. We hope you will find the book helpful in your pursuit of musical excellence.

ABOUT THE AUTHORS

Sandy Feldstein - Sandy Feldstein is a highly respected performer, composer, arranger, conductor and educator of national prominence. He is the recipient of numerous degrees, including a doctorate from Columbia University, and is an ASCAP award-winning composer. In the area of percussion, Dr. Feldstein has distinguished himself as a leader in percussion education. As past president of the Percussive Arts Society, he was cited by that group for his contribution to the world of percussion. He is a frequent guest lecturer and clinician at universities and music conventions throughout the country. Regarded as a superstar in the educational field, Sandy Feldstein's music and books are used by hundreds of thousands of young people all over the world every day. He is keenly attuned to the needs of the teaching community, and for that reason, has become an innovator in educational music.

Dave Black - Dave Black received his Bachelor of Music degree in percussion performance from California State University, Northridge. He has traveled around the world with a variety of entertainers and shows, performing and/or recording with such artists as Alan King, Robert Merrill, June Allyson, Anita O'Day and Jerry Hey. As a widely published composer/arranger, he has written with and for the bands of Louie Bellson, Sammy Nestico, Bill Watrous, Bobby Shew and Ed Shaughnessy. He is the recipient of nine ASCAP Popular Composer Awards and two Grammy participation/nomination certificates. He is the co-author of several national best-selling books, including *Alfred's Drum Method, Books 1& 2, Alfred's Beginning Drumset Method, Contemporary Brush Techniques* and *Cymbals: A Crash Course.* In addition, he has written countless articles, book and concert reviews for such magazines as *Down Beat, The Instrumentalist, Modern Drummer, Jazz Educator's Journal* and others.

The authors wish to thank the following people for their invaluable assistance: Scott Lavine, Joel Leach, Christopher Leach (model), J. Jeff Leland (photographer), John O'Reilly and Joe Vasile.

TABLE OF CONTENTS

THE SNARE DRUM

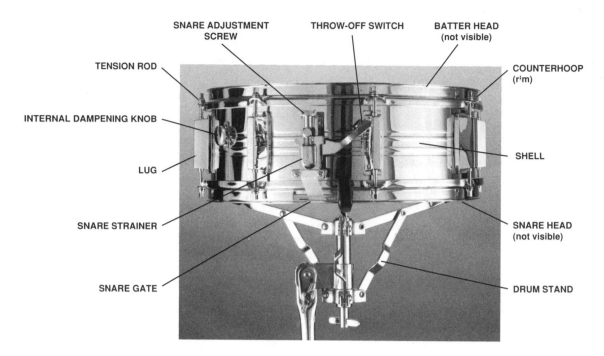

SNARE ADJUSTMENT SCREW • THROW-OFF SWITCH • BATTER HEAD (not visible) • TENSION ROD • COUNTERHOOP (rim) • INTERNAL DAMPENING KNOB • LUG • SHELL • SNARE STRAINER • SNARE HEAD (not visible) • SNARE GATE • DRUM STAND

Tuning the Snare Drum

The top head of a snare drum is referred to as the batter head. The bottom head is called the snare head. Heads are held in place by rims and can be adjusted by means of threaded rods attached to the lugs on the side of the snare drum. The number of rods and lugs attached to the snare drum depends upon the size of the drum but there are usually 8 to 10 on most drums. Adjusting these rods alters the tension of the drum heads.

When tuning the snare drum we suggest that you start with the batter side first. Tune the head by using the cross system method of tensioning. This method maintains even tensioning around the drum throughout the entire tuning process. Tap the head with a drum stick about two inches from each rod to be certain that the pitch is consistent all the way around the drum. If it is not, adjust individual tension rods as needed.

Cross tension system of tensioning

You may also tune the drum sequentially, tightening the rods as you move in a circular fashion around the drum. Tighten each screw one-half turn (or twist of the wrist) each time. Do this repeatedly until the drum head feels firm. Be sure you don't tension any lug more than the others. Tap the head with a drum stick about two inches from each rod to be certain that the pitch is consistent all the way around the drum.

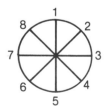

Clockwise system of tensioning

Tuning the Snare Drum (continued)

The snare head is tensioned in much the same manner as was the batter head. You may have to use one hand to lift the snares from the surface of the head while tensioning with the other hand to avoid snare rattle as you proceed. Tension the snare head firmly, but be sure that it is able to vibrate freely against the snares.

After achieving the desired pitch and tension for both heads, tap the batter head with a drumstick while adjusting the "snare adjustment screw" until the snares have been brought into contact with the snare head and the desired sound has been achieved. Be careful not to over-tighten the drum heads and the snares or you might restrict the sound of the drum. Remember, sound is produced by allowing the heads and snares of the drum to vibrate freely. Test continually by tapping the head lightly with a drumstick.

Drum Heads

The majority of drummers today use plastic drum heads exclusively. There are a wide variety of such heads on the market today; the drummer will have to choose the drum head which will best fit his/her needs. Skin heads, once the only kind available, are no longer very popular due to both price and maintenance factors.

Plastic heads become soiled after continued usage; they may be cleaned with a damp cloth and mild soap.

The Snares

Wire snares are most commonly used on concert or kit drums. They are not affected by weather conditions and require very little up-keep.

Gut snares are most commonly used on parade/field drums where a crisp sound and higher volume levels are required. Since gut snares are easily affected by weather conditions (such as humidity), extra care is required in maintaining them. Regardless of the type, snares should not be too tight; they should be adjusted so that the drum "speaks freely" and does not choke.

Maintaining Your Snare Drum

Regular cleaning of your snare drum will help prolong both the life and the quality of the drum.

Wood parts may be cleaned with a damp cloth and mild soap if necessary; mild furniture polish may be applied to wood surfaces. Metal shells and hoops may be cleaned with a damp cloth or metal polish. Pearl finishes may be cleaned with a damp cloth. Tension rods should be lubricated with Vaseline or light grease and moving parts such as the snare strainer and control arm should be lubricated with light machine oil.

6

GETTING READY TO PLAY

Holding the Sticks

There are many ways of holding drumsticks, depending on the style of drumming on which you are concentrating. The authors recommend that the beginning student start with the traditional grip. Developing the proper position and manner of holding the drumsticks is very important in the development of proper technique, attack, and control. Check periodically to make sure that the sticks are being held correctly, that the arm position is as it should be and that the general position of the body is correct. Practicing in front of a mirror can be helpful in this regard.

The Right Hand

The stick should be thought of as a natural extension of the arm. 1) The stick is gripped between the thumb and first joint of the index finger, one third of the distance from the butt end of the stick. The other fingers will be used to help control the stick. 2) Close the other fingers loosely around the stick. 3) Turn the hand so that the back of the hand is facing upward when playing. The stick should be in an approximate line with the wrist and arm.

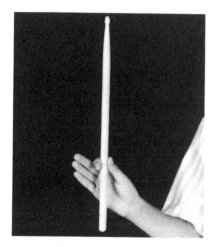 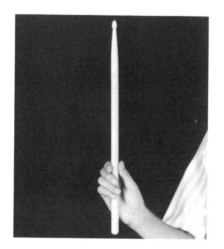 

The Left Hand

1) Place the stick in the socket between the thumb and first finger, with one third of the stick (from the butt end) extending behind the hand. The grip should be just tight enough to cause a slight drag if one were to try to pull the stick from the hand. 2) The first two fingers should rest lightly on top of the stick (the first more than the second) to act as a guide. The stick should rest across the third finger which will act as a support. The fourth finger should rest against the third finger.

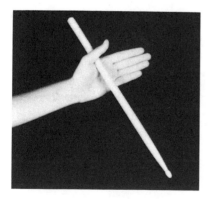 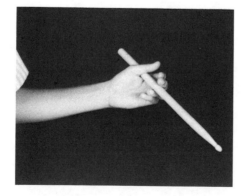 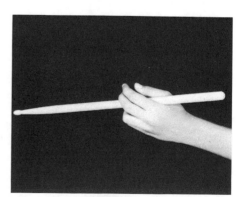

Matched Grip

In both hands, the sticks are gripped between the thumb and first joint of the index finger, one third of the distance from the butt end of the stick (see right hand grip description above for details).

Striking the Drum

When resting on the drum head, the sticks should approximate a 90 degree angle. They should strike near (but not on) the center of the drum head. The space in which they strike should be no larger than 1½ to 2 inches in diameter. Since the pitch of the drum varies considerably as you move from the center of the drum head to the rim, it is important that each stick be kept an equal distance from the center of the head so that an even tone is produced. (There may be times, however, when you will want to play a passage "near the edge.")

Sound is produced by striking the top head. This sets the air inside the drum in motion, which causes the bottom head and snares to vibrate. Because of this, the sticks must be allowed to rebound from the head as quickly as possible.

THE STROKE is produced by a turn of the wrist in a down-up motion.
1. Place the tip of the stick on the head.
2. Turn the wrist so the tip of the stick is as far away from the head as possible.
3. Play the stroke (down-up) striking the head and returning immediately to the up position.

1.  2., 3.

1.  2., 3.

When alternating strokes, the right (left) stick strikes the drum and rebounds to a position approximately two inches above the head. When the left (right) stick comes down, the right stick goes from the low position to the full up position.

THE BASS DRUM

The bass drum is the largest member of the drum family. Its main function is to hold a steady tempo and to help with phrasing and accents. The bass drum should be positioned so that the music stand and the director may be seen in a straight line.

The Size of the Bass Drum

The size of the bass drum should be determined by the type of playing and by the size of the musical organization in which it is to be used. The depth of the drum should not be over one-half of the diameter of the head.

Tuning the Bass Drum

It's important that the tension be equalized around the entire circumference to obtain the best tone. This is accomplished in much the same manner as with snare drum tuning.

The tone of the bass drum should be "dark" and low in pitch. If the head is too loose, it will vibrate lifelessly; if too tight, it will ring too much. Both heads should be at approximately the same pitch for maximum resonance.

Where to Strike the Drum

When struck in the exact center, the drum head produces a "dull thud;" the area near the rim produces a high pitched ringing tone. The best playing spot is about halfway between the center and the edge of the drum. This may vary depending on the musical setting and the size of the ensemble.

The Bass Drum Beater

There are many types of bass drum beaters available; since the beater affects the drum's tone significantly, it is very important that careful thought be given to the selection process.

Although the common double-headed lamb's wool beater is acceptable, many people feel it does not produce the best tone. A somewhat heavier single-headed beater will generally prove superior.

The Stroke

The proper bass drum stroke is achieved by striking the head with a direct, horizontal blow, immediately bringing the beater back to its starting position. Be sure to contact the drum half-way between the center and the edge to obtain the fullest sound.

THE CYMBALS

Hand Cymbals

For medium and large size bands, a matched pair of cymbals 16" to 18" in diameter will be most satisfactory.

Leather straps with leather or lamb's wool disks are the most popular devices for holding cymbals. Wooden handles are not recommended, since they will deaden the tone and may cause the cymbals to crack.

Playing the Cymbals

The cymbals are brought together with a glancing blow. The left hand (for a right-handed player) remains stationary, while the right hand executes the stroke. In concert situations, this action is repeated for successive blows.

In the marching band, it's sometimes acceptable to use an alternating up and down motion to minimize fatigue.

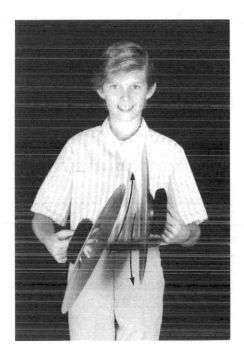

To muffle (or choke) the cymbals and stop the vibrations, the player draws the cymbals against the chest or forearms.

Cymbal knots should be tied correctly and checked frequently. Tie it again (directly on top of the first knot) for added security.

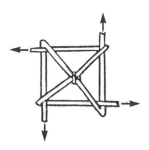

ELEMENTS OF MUSIC

Whole—Half—Quarter Notes

The duration of musical sounds (long or short) is indicated by different types of notes.

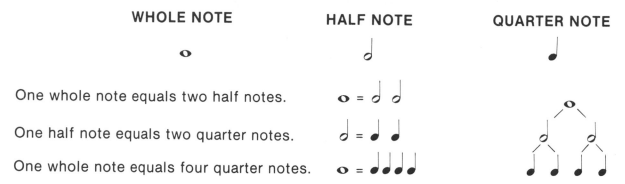

| WHOLE NOTE | HALF NOTE | QUARTER NOTE |

One whole note equals two half notes.

One half note equals two quarter notes.

One whole note equals four quarter notes.

Measure—Bar Lines—Double Bar Lines

Music is divided into equal parts called **MEASURES**.

BAR LINES indicate the beginning and end of measures.

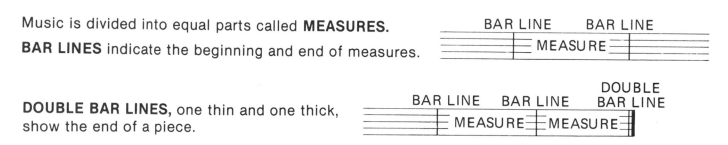

BAR LINE   BAR LINE

MEASURE

DOUBLE BAR LINES, one thin and one thick, show the end of a piece.

DOUBLE
BAR LINE   BAR LINE   BAR LINE

MEASURE   MEASURE

Time Signatures and Note Values

TIME SIGNATURES are placed at the beginning of a piece of music. They contain two numbers that show the number of beats (or counts) in each measure and the kind of note that receives one beat.

$\frac{4}{4}$ The top number shows the number of beats (or counts) in each measure.
The bottom number shows what kind of note gets one beat.

$\frac{4}{4}$ means four beats in each measure.
means a quarter note (♩) gets one beat.

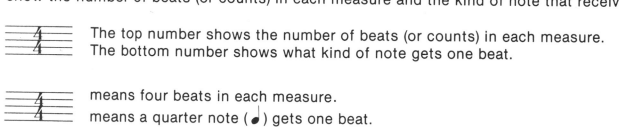

in $\frac{4}{4}$ time, a whole note receives four beats.

A half note receives two beats.

A quarter note receives one beat.

At the beginning of each line of music there is a clef sign. Unpitched percussion music uses the neutral (‖) clef.

METRONOME—A device which produces clicks and/or light flashes to indicate the tempo of the music. For instance, ♩ = 120 means that the metronome will click 120 times in a minute and each click will, in this case, represent a quarter note.

TEMPO—The rate of speed of a musical piece or passage. Tempo may be indicated by a musical term, or by an exact metronome marking.

YOU ARE NOW READY TO PLAY

Things to remember:

Time Signatures and Note Values

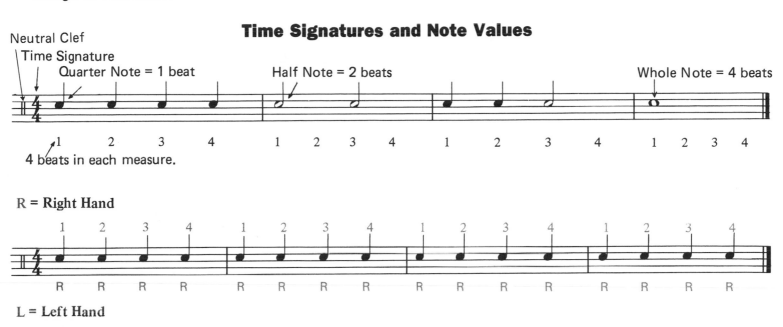

R = Right Hand

L = Left Hand

When alternating strokes, be sure to bring the left stick tip up as the right hand comes down, and the right stick tip up as the left hand comes down.

Repeat Signs

Two dots placed before a double bar line ⫸ means go back to the beginning and play again.

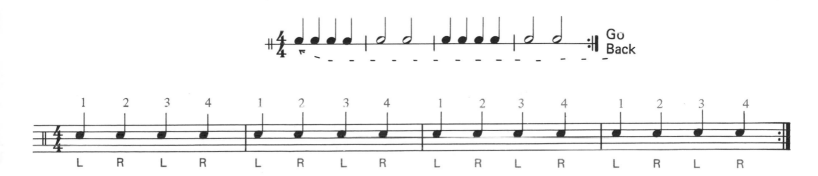

Some music in this method will contain Snare Drum and Bass Drum parts. It is suggested that each student practice both parts and develop the techniques of each instrument. The two parts may be played by one player, executing the bass drum part with the toe of his/her right foot as one would when playing at the drum set. The two parts may also be played as a duet by a snare drummer and bass drummer.

LESSON 1
Quarter Notes, Quarter Rests

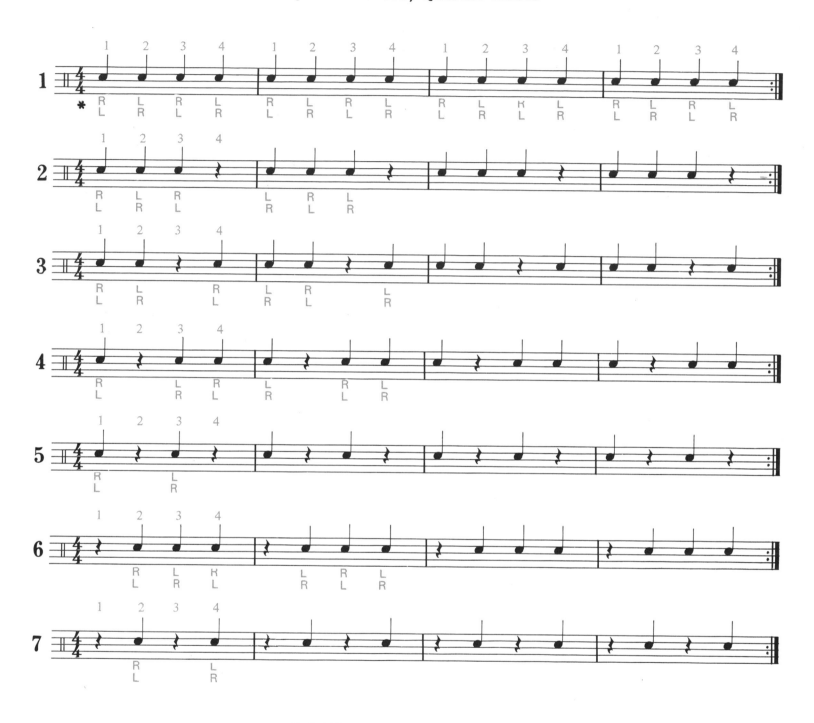

COMBINATION STUDY

*Throughout this method all exercises should be practiced beginning with both the right hand and the left hand.

LESSON 2
Eighth Notes, Quarter Notes

An **EIGHTH NOTE** looks like a quarter note with a flag added to its stem:

Two or more **EIGHTH NOTES** are joined together by a beam:

COMBINATION STUDY

* 𝅗𝅥 =half note = two beats

LESSON 3
Quarter Notes, Quarter Rests, Eighth Notes

COMBINATION STUDY

* ▬ - half rest = two beats of silence

Dynamics

Dynamic signs indicate how loudly or softly music should be played.

The symbol f forte—means: loud

The symbol p piano—means: soft

A crescendo ⟍ means: gradually get louder

A decrescendo ⟍ means: gradually get softer

𝄎. = repeat previous measure

▬ = *whole rest* = 4 beats of silence

First and Second Endings

The repeat sign tells you to go back to the beginning. On the repeat, skip the first ending and play the second ending.

PLAY THIS ENDING
FIRST TIME ONLY   SECOND TIME ONLY

SOLO #1

Moderato ♩ = 120

* 𝅘 = play on rim

LESSON 4
Eighth Notes, Quarter Notes, Eighth Rests

♪ = eighth rest

COMBINATION STUDY

LESSON 5
Eighth Notes, Eighth Rests

COMBINATION STUDY

LESSON 6
Dotted Half Notes, Dotted Quarter Notes

A dot (•) placed after a note increases its value by one-half the value of the original note.

COMBINATION STUDY

SOLO #2

The symbol ff **fortissimo**—means: very loud
The symbol pp **pianissimo**—means: very soft

D.S. = **Dal Segno**—means: go back to the sign (𝄋)
Fine = the end
If we put them together, we get:
D.S. al Fine = Go back to the sign (𝄋) and play to the end, indicated by **Fine.**

* Repeats are traditionally not observed on a D.S.

LESSON 7
Sixteenth Notes, Eighth Notes, Quarter Notes

A **sixteenth note** looks like an eighth note with a second flag added to its stem:

Two or more **sixteenth notes** are joined together by two beams.

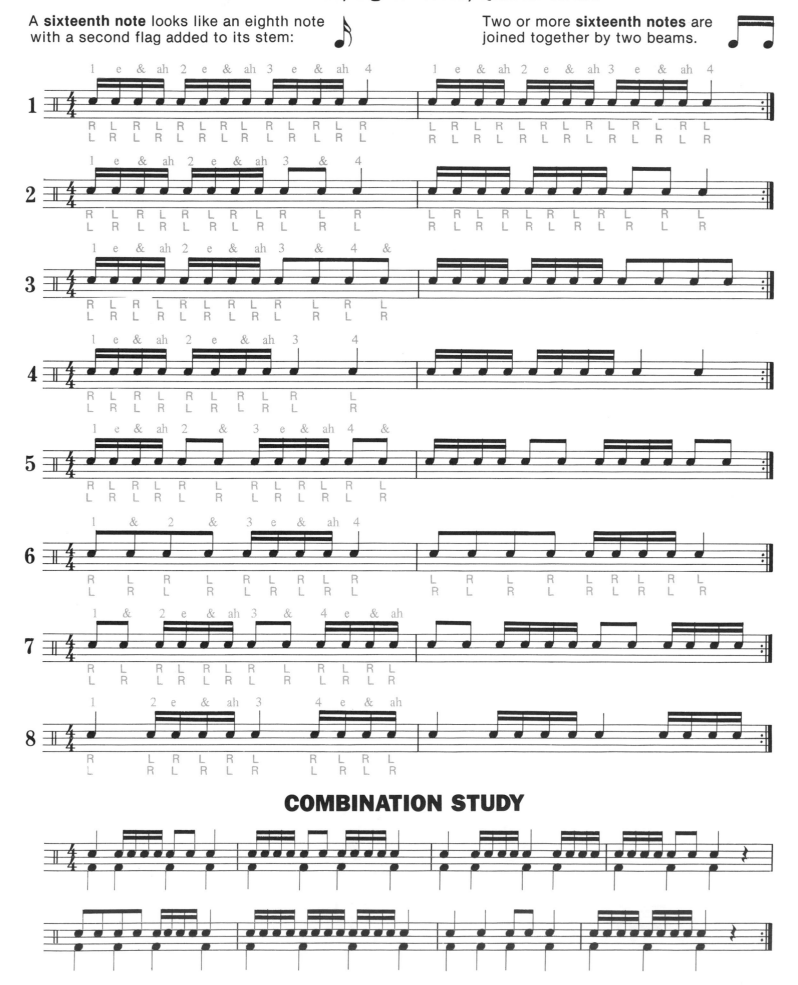

COMBINATION STUDY

LESSON 8
Sixteenth Notes, Eighth Notes

COMBINATION STUDY

SOLO #3

> = **Accent**—means: play the note a little louder
The symbol *mp* **mezzo piano**—means: moderately soft
The symbol *mf* **mezzo forte**—means: moderately loud

f-p = play *f* the first time, *p* on the repeat.

LESSON 9
Sixteenth Notes, Eighth Notes, Eighth Rests

COMBINATION STUDY

LESSON 10
Sixteenth Notes, Sixteenth Rests

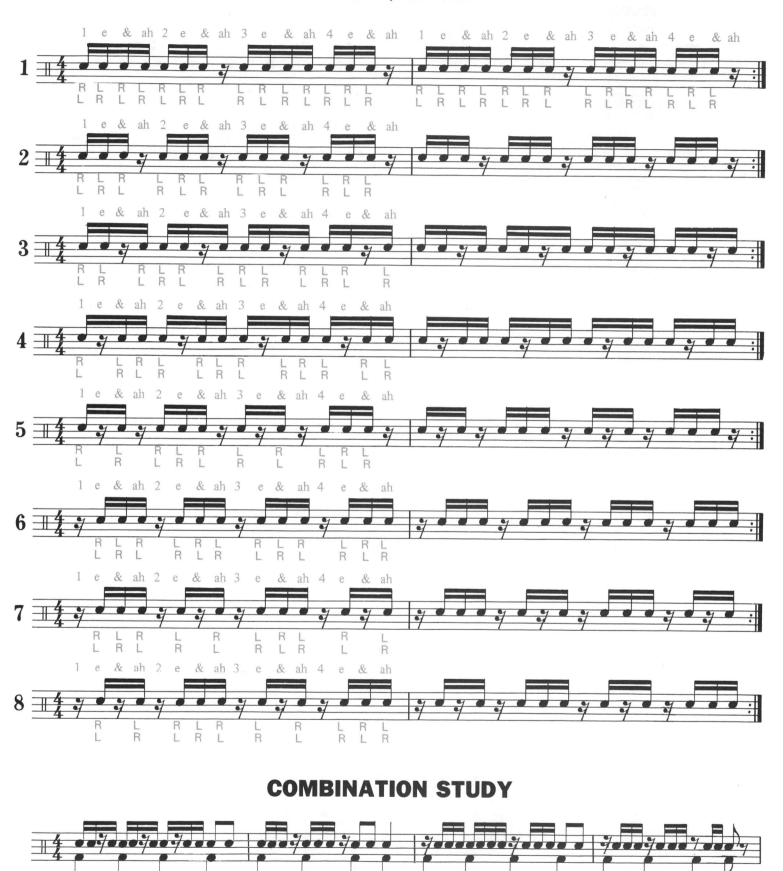

COMBINATION STUDY

SOLO #4

D.C. = ***Da Capo***—means: go back to the beginning. Sometimes a composition ends with a separate closing section. This is called a ***Coda*** and is indicated by a Coda sign (𝄌).

If we combine Coda with D.C., we get:
D.C. al Coda = Go back to the beginning and play to the Coda sign (𝄌), then skip to the Coda to end the piece.

= repeat the previous two measures.

LESSON 11
Dotted Eighth and Sixteenth Notes

A dot (·) placed after a note increases its value by one-half the value of the original note.

Example:

COMBINATION STUDY

SOLO #5

LESSON 12
2/4 Time

The top number shows the number of beats (or counts) in each measure.
The bottom number shows what kind of note gets one beat.

means two beats in each measure.
means quarter note gets one beat.

COMBINATION STUDY

SOLO #6

* R.S. = rimshot: Place the tip of one stick on the drum head. Strike that stick in the middle with the other stick.

LESSON 13
Eighth Notes, Sixteenth Notes, Eighth Rests

COMBINATION STUDY

LESSON 14
Sixteenth Notes, Sixteenth Rests

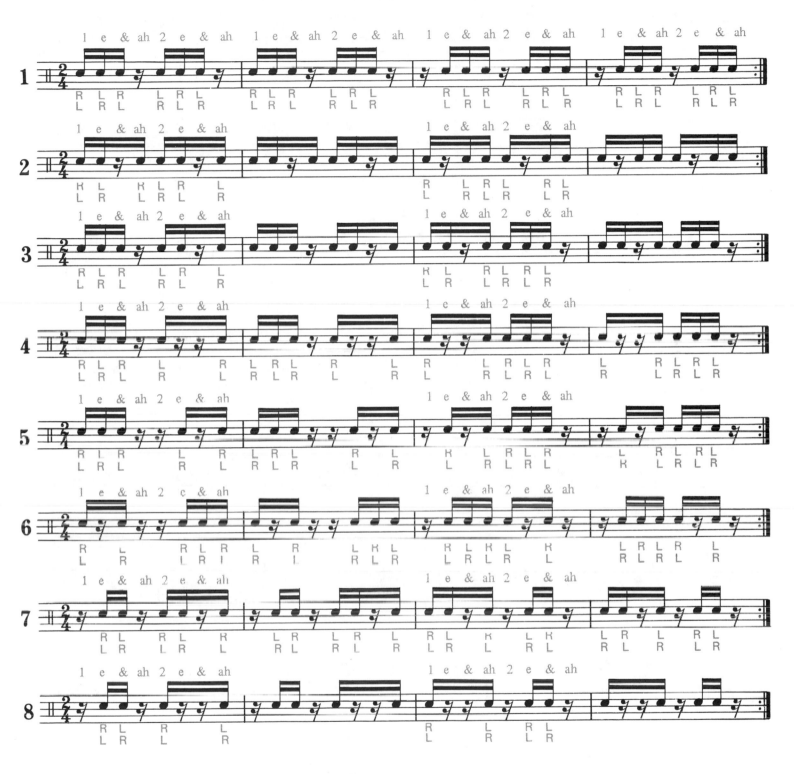

COMBINATION STUDY

SOLO #7

SOLO #8

LESSON 15
3/4 Time

In 3/4 time there are 3 beats in each measure and a quarter note receives one beat.

$\frac{3}{4}$ means three beats in each measure.
means quarter note gets one beat.

COMBINATION STUDY

LESSON 16
Sixteenth Notes, Eighth Notes

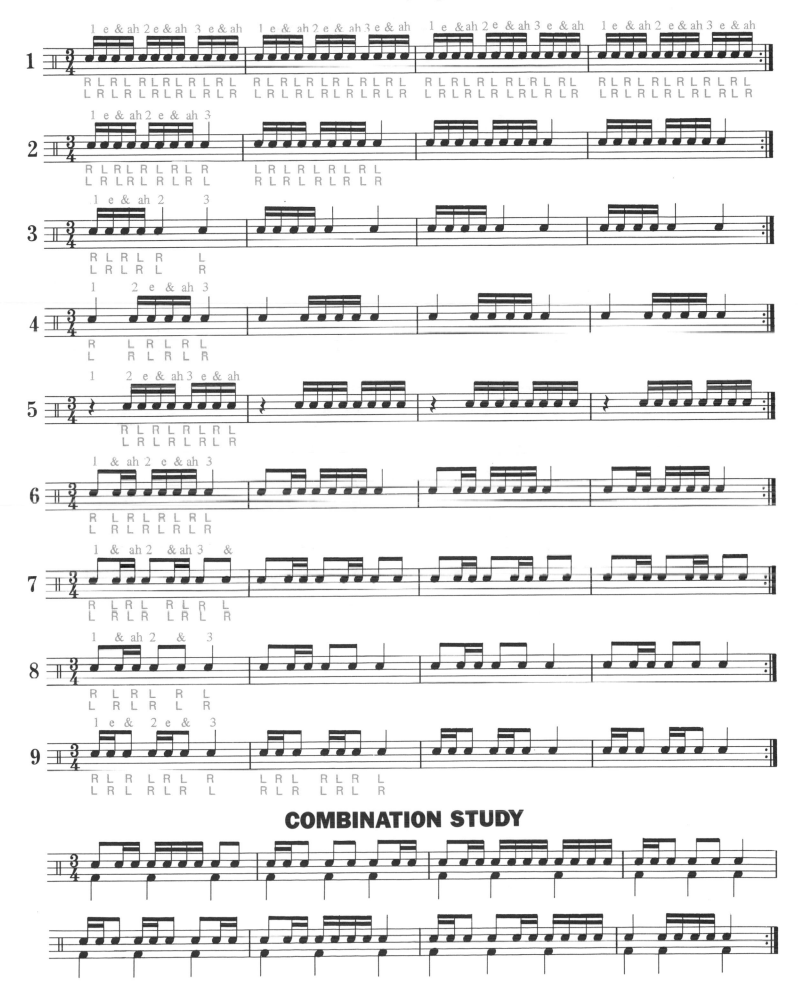

COMBINATION STUDY

SOLO #9

LESSON #17
The Roll

There are two types of rolls used by snare drummers: the double stroke and the multiple bounce or "buzz" roll. Rolls are indicated by three diagonal lines drawn through the stems of a note.

Example:

The double stroke roll, most commonly used by marching bands, is executed by playing two strokes with each hand. The first stroke (primary stroke) is executed by the wrist, while the second (secondary stroke) is a bounce produced by using the fingers. Both must be controlled and of equal volume.

The multiple bounce or unmeasured roll which is most often used by concert and drum-set drummers, is comprised of multiple bounces on each stick—often as many as 5-9 per stroke. In order to produce an even multiple bounce roll, make sure that each stick strikes the head in the same manner to achieve matching sounds. With time and practice the student will be able to develop a smooth and sustained multiple bounce roll.

It is possible to use multiple bounce rolls in all situations, including the Sousa marches on the following pages. Your teacher will show you how to use this technique.

LESSON 18
The 5-Stroke Roll

The 5-stroke roll consists of a series of 2 double strokes followed by a single stroke: Example: RRLLR or LLRRL. (At slow speeds, the strokes are executed individually.)

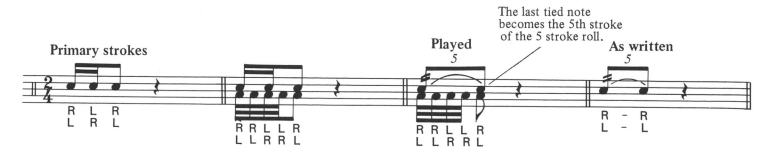

When playing 5-stroke rolls, the hand that begins the roll will also end it.

COMBINATION STUDY

SOLO #10

LESSON 19
The 9-Stroke Roll

The 9-stroke roll consists of a series of 4 double strokes followed by a single stroke.
Example: RRLLRRLLR or LLRRLLRRL. (At slow speeds, the strokes are executed individually.)

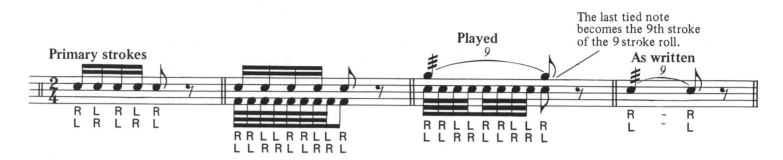

When playing 9-stroke rolls, the hand that begins the roll will also end it.

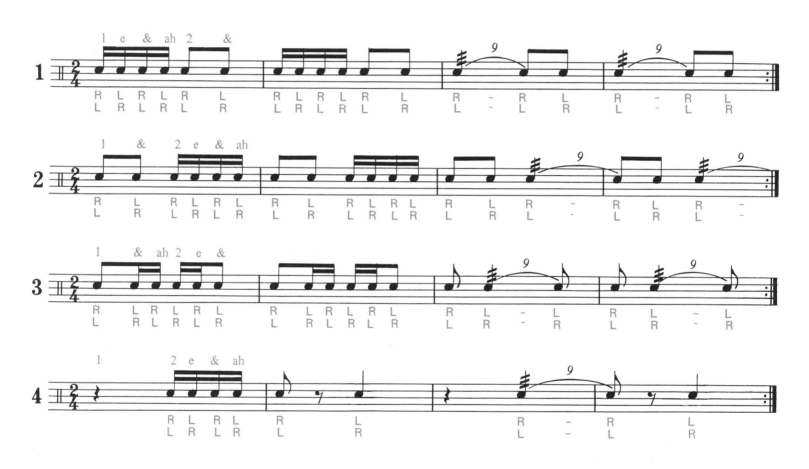

COMBINATION STUDY

SOLO #11

SOLO #12

LESSON 20
The 13-Stroke Roll

The 13-stroke roll consists of a series of 6 double strokes followed by a single stroke.
Example: RRLLRRLLRRLLR or LLRRLLRRLLRRL. (At slow speeds, the strokes are executed individually.)

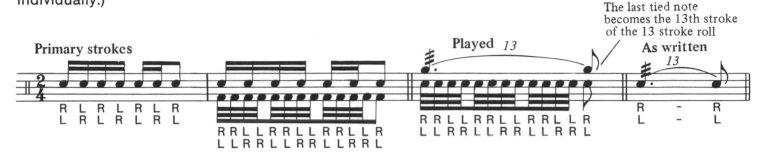

When playing 13-stroke rolls, the hand that begins the roll will also end it.

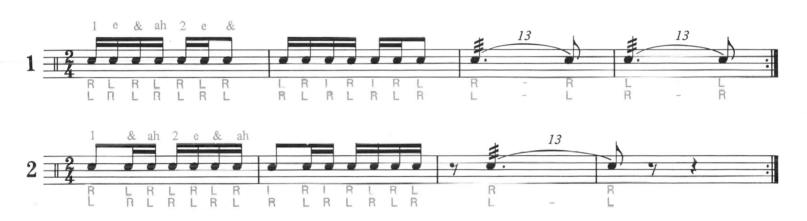

The 17-Stroke Roll

The 17-stroke roll consists of 8 double strokes followed by a single stroke.
Example: RRLLRRLLRRLLRRLLR or LLRRLLRRLLRRLLRRL. (At slow speeds, the strokes are executed individually.)

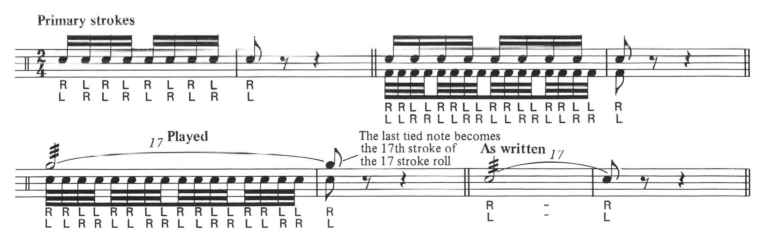

When playing 17-stroke rolls, the hand that begins the roll will also end it.

SOLO #13

THE U.S. FIELD ARTILLERY MARCH

SOUSA
Arr. Feldstein/Black

LESSON 21
3/4 Time, Rolls

COMBINATION STUDY

SOLO #14

LESSON 22
Triplets

A triplet is a group of three notes of equal value, usually played in the place of one note. A triplet will have the numeral "3" placed above or beneath the center note.

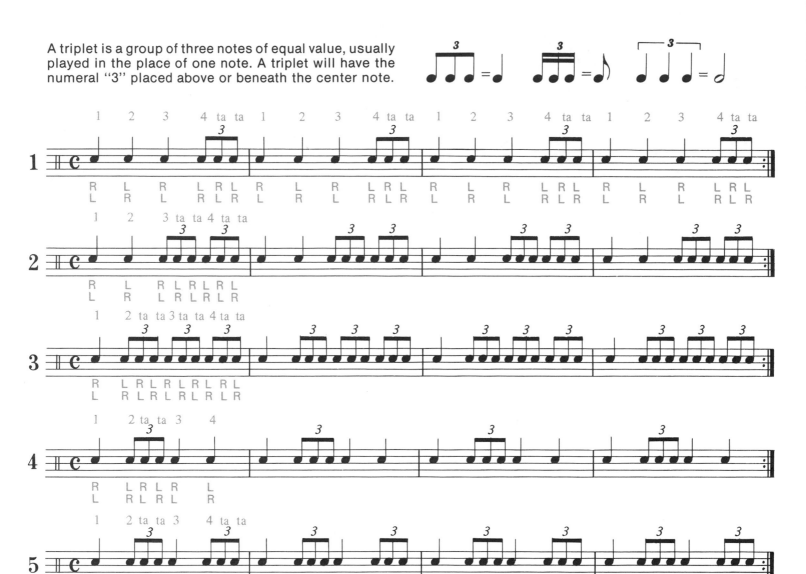

COMBINATION STUDY

LESSON 23
Sixteenth Note Triplets, Eighth Notes

COMBINATION STUDY

SOLO #15

LESSON 24
The 7-Stroke Roll

Because the 7-stroke roll starts and ends on opposite hands, it is usually not alternated as were the 5, 9,13 and 17-stroke rolls. It most often begins with the left hand and ends with the right and is frequently used as a substitute for the 5-stroke roll.

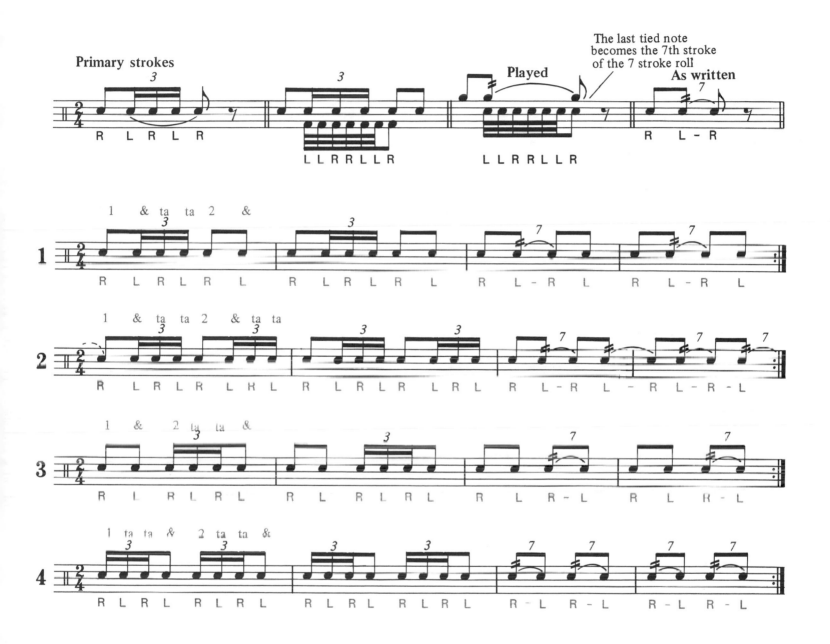

COMBINATION STUDY

SOLO #16

LESSON 25
Alla Breve or "Cut-Time"

The time signature for Alla Breve (cut time) is $\frac{2}{2}$ or ₵ . There are two beats or counts in each measure of cut time and a half note receives one beat or count.

Example: ₵ or $\frac{2}{2}$ = Beats (or Counts) in each measure.
            ₵ or $\frac{2}{2}$ = (Half) note or rest receives one beat (or Count).

LESSON 26
Eighth Notes, Quarter Notes

COMBINATION STUDY

SOLO #17

HANDS ACROSS THE SEA

SOUSA
Arr. Feldstein/Black

*Play the 2nd & 4th quarter notes a little louder than the 1st & 3rd.

LESSON 27

The Flam

The flam is a combination of a small note (grace note) and a main note. Its purpose is to produce a broader sound (tenuto). The sticks do not strike the head at the same time, but must strike close enough so that they will almost sound as one stroke. If the grace note is played by the left hand, the main note is played by the right and vice versa. The name of the flam is designated according to the hand that strikes the main note.

The flam is not necessarily an accented note and should be played at a normal volume unless the main note is accompanied by an accent.

Example:

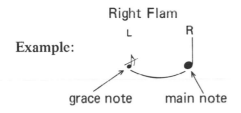

Right Flam

grace note   main note

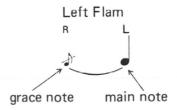

Left Flam

grace note   main note

Position for right hand flam.

Position for left-hand flam.

The hand playing the grace note starts approximately two inches above the head. After playing the grace note, the stick moves to the up position. The stick playing the main note rebounds to approximately two inches above the head, ready to play the grace note of the next flam.

LESSON 27
(Continued)

COMBINATION STUDY

SOLO #18

LESSON 28
Flam Rudiments

Flam Accent
(also called Flam Accent No. 1)
A flam accent combines a flam with two other single strokes. Flam accents are played alternately.

Flam Tap
A flam tap is a flam combined with a second stroke, making one group of double strokes.

Flamacue
A flamacue is a combination of two flams and single strokes with an accent placed on the second note.

COMBINATION STUDY

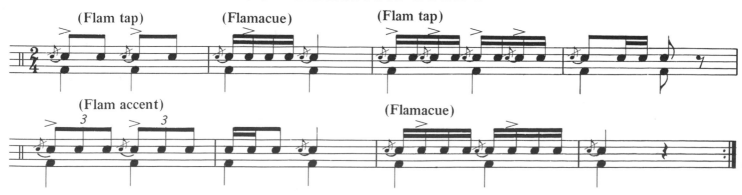

SOLO #19

Andante ♩ = 100

*Use Flam Tap, Flamacue & Flam Accent stickings where possible.

THE THUNDERER

$\frac{2}{}$ = rest for two measures

SOUSA
Arr. Feldstein/Black

*This roll is often played as a 7 stroke roll to add excitment to the end of the piece.

LESSON 29
6/8 Time

In 6/8 time there are six beats in each measure and an eighth note receives one beat.

6 means six beats in each measure.
8 means an eighth note gets one beat.

COMBINATION STUDY

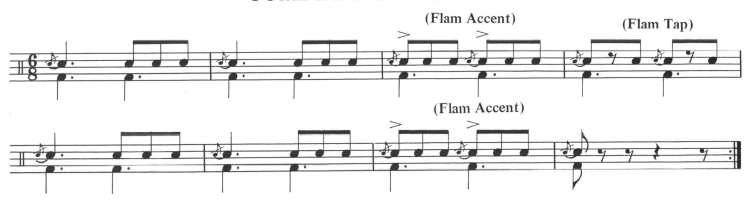

LESSON 30
Eighth Notes, Sixteenth Notes, Eighth Rests

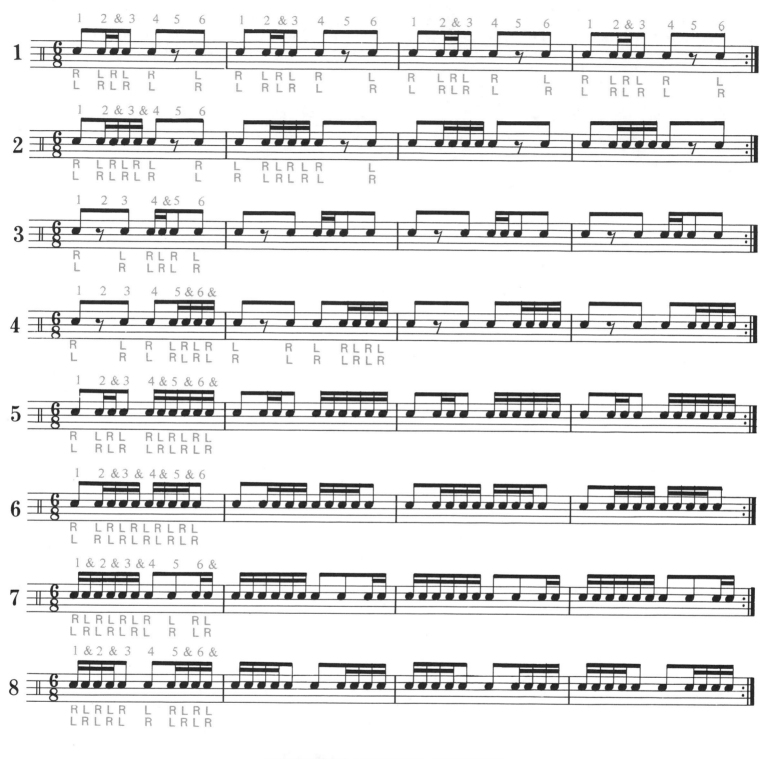

COMBINATION STUDY

LESSON 31
Rolls in 6/8

The 5-Stroke Roll

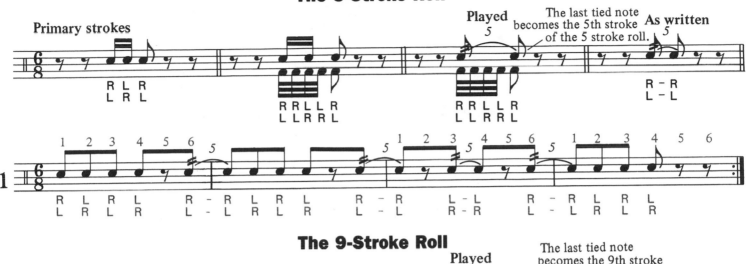

The 9-Stroke Roll

The 13-Stroke Roll

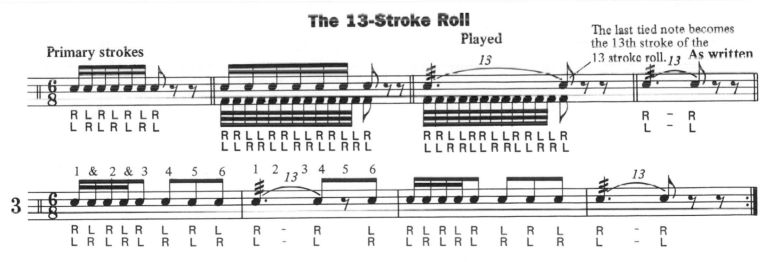

COMBINATION STUDY

SOLO #20

*Use Flam Accent and Flam Tap stickings where possible.

LESSON 32
6/8 "in 2"

When 6/8 time is played at fast
tempos, it is usually counted "in 2".

COMBINATION STUDY

LESSON 33
6/8 "In 2" with Rolls

When 6/8 is played "in 2", the primary strokes of the rolls become eighth notes.

The 5-Stroke Roll

The 7-Stroke Roll

The 13-Stroke Roll

COMBINATION STUDY

THE LIBERTY BELL

SOUSA
Arr. Feldstein/Black

*Play 1st & 2nd endings on D.S.

LESSON 34
The Drag
(sometimes referred to as a 3-stroke ruff)

The drag (or 3-stroke ruff) consists of two grace notes and a main note. The two grace notes are played softer than the main note. The drag may begin with either hand.

The 3-Stroke Ruff

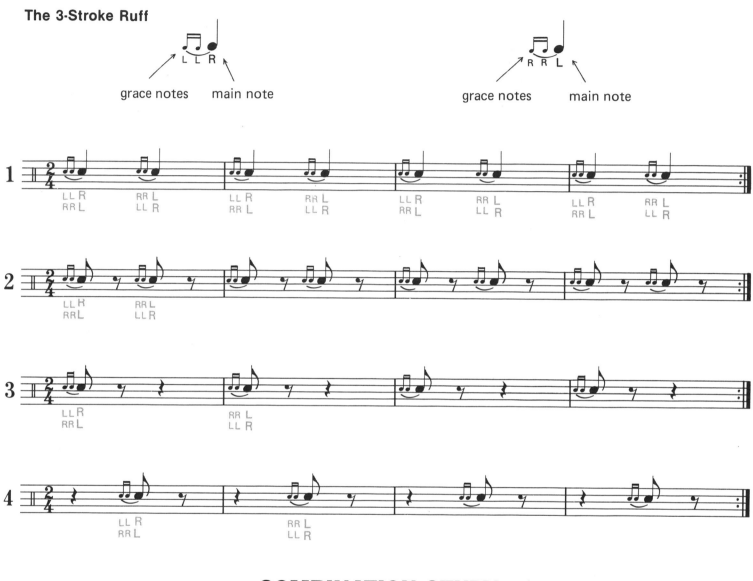

COMBINATION STUDY

LESSON 35
The Ruff

A ruff is a combination of two or more grace notes and a main note. The grace notes are played softer than the main note. The ruff may begin with either hand.

The 4-Stroke Ruff

The 4-stroke ruff consists of three grace notes and a main note. The 4-stroke ruff is played with single strokes rather than bounces and may begin with either hand.

The 4-Stroke Ruff

COMBINATION STUDY

SOLO #21

LESSON 36
Syncopation

Syncopation occurs when a temporary displacement of the regular metrical accent occurs, causing the emphasis to shift from a strong accent to a weak accent.

COMBINATION STUDY

LESSON 37
Syncopation in 3/4 Time, 2/4 Time

COMBINATION STUDY

SOLO #22

D.S. = **Dal Segno**—means: go back to the sign (𝄋)
Sometimes a composition ends with a separate
closing section. This is called a *Coda* and is
indicated by a *Coda* sign (⊕).

If we combine *Coda* with *D.S.*, we get:
D.S. al Coda = Go back to the sign (𝄋) and play to
the *Coda* sign (⊕), then skip to the *Coda* to end the
piece.

LESSON 38
Tied Notes

A curved line is sometimes used to connect two notes which appear on the same line or space. This is called a tie. The first note is played, while the time value of the second note is added to the first note.

COMBINATION STUDY

LESSON 39
Tied Notes, Rolls

COMBINATION STUDY

SOLO #23